SCOTT FORESMAN READING STREET
Family Talk

GRADE 2

COMMON CORE EDITION ©

ISBN-13: 978-0-328-68637-7
ISBN-10:   0-328-68637-9
12 16

Glenview, Illinois

Boston, Massachusetts

Chandler, Arizona

Upper Saddle River, New Jersey

ALWAYS LEARNING

PEARSON

Table of Contents

Unit 4–Our Changing World

Unit 5–Responsibility

Unit 6–Traditions

Date _____

Dear _____,

Your child has just begun a new unit on Reading Street! The name of this unit is Exploration. Over the next several weeks, our class will be reading about and discussing the concept of exploration. Throughout this unit, we will be exploring neighborhoods, outer space, deserts, and other exciting places.

The Big Question for this unit is *What can we learn from exploring new places and things?* As we focus on this question at school, take opportunities to emphasize it at home as well. Use conversational opportunities during meals, play time, and car rides to talk with your child about the concept of exploration.

In this issue of *Family Talk,* you will find conversation starters, family projects and activities, and concept-related vocabulary and questions. All of these will help you and your child build understanding of this unit's concept.

Have fun!

Sincerely,

_____

What can we learn from exploring new places and things?

Concept Conversation Starters

To help your child identify different ways of exploring, ask him or her these questions and talk about the answers.

- Let's explore a room in our home. How big is it? What is in the room? Do we learn anything new about the room?
- How do we explore places that we are visiting for the first time?
- What can we explore in the park or on a walk around our neighborhood?
- What can you explore in your classroom at school?
- How does exploring the world around you help you learn?
- How is reading a story together like exploring someplace new?
- How is playing hide-and-seek like exploring? What do you learn as you play hide-and-seek?

Family Project

Hold hands and take a family walk to a park or another place in your community. As you walk, point out things of nature, including plants, animals, streams, and rocks. Look at the people around you and the buildings, roadways, and playgrounds they have constructed. Take photographs if you can. When you return home, talk about what you learned as you explored your community. If you took photographs, have your child help you write captions for them and place them in an album. Alternatively, sit down with your child and together draw pictures of things you saw. Post the pictures on a bulletin board or staple them together in a homemade booklet titled "Exploring Our Community."

Weekly Questions and Word Lists

	The Twin Club	Exploring Space with an Astronaut	Henry and Mudge and the Starry Night	A Walk in the Desert	The Strongest One
Weekly Question	What can we learn by exploring different communities?	What can we learn by exploring space?	What can we discover by exploring nature?	What can we learn by exploring the desert?	How does exploration help us find answers?
Amazing Words	investigate, rural, urban	journey, orbit, universe	detective, wildlife, fascinating	arid, precipitation, landform	inquire, exhibit, satisfaction
More Concept Vocabulary	search, neighborhood	astronauts, space, moon	hiking, stars, rivers	saguaro, hot, cold, sand	answers, world, skills

Selection Summaries and Questions

The Twin Club

Jorge and his cousin Juan spend summers at their grandma's house. After someone in Grandma's hometown thinks the cousins are twins, the cousins decide to start the Twin Club. In the Twin Club, Jorge and Juan do everything together, including exploring the small town Grandma lives in. At the end of the summer, the cousins return to their homes. To keep the Twin Club going, they write e-mails to one another and plan for the next summer's explorations.

- Juan and Jorge explore their grandmother's small town. What have you explored in your community? Where do you like to go? What can you learn from exploring your community?

- At home, Juan explores the fields and a neighbor's barn. What would you like to explore on a farm?

- Jorge sends an e-mail that descibes his neighborhood. What would you tell about your neighborhood in an e-mail?

Exploring Space with an Astronaut

Astronauts soar into space aboard a space shuttle. They are ready to explore ways to live and work in space.

Every shuttle flight has a crew of astronauts led by a pilot. Eileen Collins was the pilot on one flight. Eileen's crew flew the shuttle and did experiments. One very important job they had was testing an X-ray telescope and releasing it into space.

Think about what it is like to be an astronaut. They need to know math and science. They probably enjoy exploring new places. Perhaps you would like to be an astronaut someday.

- Would you like to be an astronaut? Tell why or why not.

- Astronauts do many different jobs, including science experiments, as they travel through space. Why do you think they do science experiments in space?

Henry and Mudge

Henry's family and their dog, Mudge, go on a camping trip. Before the trip, Henry thinks about all the animals they will see. He worries that they might see a bear. But he should not have worried. They see waterfalls and a rainbow as they hike along a trail. And they see fish and deer, but no bears!

As the family enjoys the sights and sounds on their hike, Mudge does some exploring of his own, sniffing and pawing things around him. That night the family looks up at the star-filled sky. Then Henry snuggles with Mudge and falls asleep thinking about the wonders of nature.

- Henry and his family explore nature on a camping trip. How can you explore nature where you live?

- Can you see lots of stars where you live?

- Where would you like to hike? What could you learn about nature as you hiked through this place?

A Walk in the Desert

Deserts are dry areas of land that can be found all over the world. They are exciting places to explore.

Saguaro cactuses, tall plants that grow in the desert, store water in their stems. Many animals live inside these cactuses. Desert animals have adapted to life there, such as protecting themselves from the hot sun, hunting for food, and escaping from enemies. Many animals there hunt for food at night.

- Describe how a desert is like where you live. Describe how it is different from where you live.

- What kinds of supplies would you put in your backpack before you headed off to explore a desert?

- If you were exploring a desert, what might you see there?

The Strongest One

Little Red Ant wonders about the world around him. One thing he wants to know is who in the world was the strongest. Little Red Ant decides to leave the other ants and set out from his home beneath Big Rock. He will search for the answer to his question. As he ventures out to explore his world, Little Red Ant asks everyone he sees who is the strongest. He asks Snow, Sun, Wind, House, Mouse, Cat, Stick, Fire, Water, Deer, Arrow, and Big Rock the question. Each gives Little Red Ant a different answer. Big Rock's answer even said Little Red Ants were the strongest!

Little Red Ant thinks about the many answers to the question. When he returns home, he tells the other ants what he has learned. Little Red Ant has learned that everything can be stronger than something else!

- Little Red Ant asks questions to learn about the world around him. How does asking questions help you learn?

- Little Red Ant gets different answers from everyone. He uses the different answers to decide that everyone is stronger than someone else. Have you ever used answers to questions to make decisions? How did the answers help you make the decision?

- Stories can help you explore ideas and learn lessons. What lesson can you learn from this story?

Date _____

Dear _____,

Your child has just begun a new unit on Reading Street! The name of this unit is Working Together. Over the next several weeks, our class will be reading about and discussing the concept of working together. Throughout this unit, we will learn how cooperation can help rescues someone, change history, make products, and accomplish other exciting team efforts.

The Big Question for this unit is *How can we work together?* As we focus on this question at school, take opportunities to emphasize it at home as well. Use conversational opportunities during meals, play time, and car rides to talk with your child about the concept of working together.

In this issue of *Family Talk,* you will find conversation starters, family projects and activities, and concept-related vocabulary and questions. All of these will help you and your child build understanding of this unit's concept.

Have fun!

Sincerely,

_____

How can we work together?

Concept Conversation Starters

To help your child learn ways working together helps everyone, ask him or her these questions and talk about the answers.

- Think of a project we have done together. How did we work together? Did we have fun working together?
- Firefighters work together. How does this make their work easier?
- Let's write the names of some jobs where people work together. What kind of jobs do they do?
- What chores do you have? Do you sometimes have help doing your chores? How does having help make chores easier to do?

Family Project

Choose a chore that your child can help you do, such as washing and drying dishes, setting the table, dusting the furniture, collecting and taking out the trash, putting laundered clothes away, and so on. Ask your child for help, and as you work together, talk about how the job is easier and more fun when you work together to get it done. Discuss other ways that the family members can help each other.

Weekly Questions and Word Lists

	Tara and Tiree, Fearless Friends	Abraham Lincoln	Scarcity	The Bremen Town Musicians	One Good Turn Deserves Another
Weekly Question	How can we help each other in dangerous situations?	How has working together changed history?	How can we work together to meet people's needs?	Why is it a good idea to work together?	How can we work together to solve problems?
Amazing Words	courageous, instinct, hazard	ingenious, participate, significant	consumers, decisions, producers	partnership, solution, depend	conflict, resolve, deserve
More Concept Vocabulary	frozen, abandoned	identify, honest, slavery	resources, enough	talent, famous	agree, favor

Selection Summaries and Questions

Tara and Tiree, Fearless Friends

Jim has two dogs, Tara and Tiree. Jim and his dogs like to take long walks in the winter and then return to their warm home. One winter day Jim and the dogs walk out on an ice-covered lake. The ice breaks, and Jim falls into the freezing water. Tiree tries to help Jim out of the water, but she falls in too. Then Tara tries to help, but Jim is too heavy for Tara to pull out of the ice. Tiree walks on Jim's back to get out of the water. Together, the two dogs pull Jim out and save his life.

- Tara and Tiree work together to get Jim out of the water. Think of a time you worked with someone. What did you do? How did working together make the task easier?

- Some people have jobs as rescue workers. Name some kinds of rescue workers. How do they work together to rescue people?

Abraham Lincoln

Classmates accidently tear a map of the country. Their teacher uses the incident to lead into the story of Abraham Lincoln and how he worked with others to unite a nation torn apart by war.

Lincoln was born in Kentucky in 1809. He was a hard-working boy who helped do the work on the family farm. As an adult, Lincoln became known as Honest Abe when he was working in a store and walked many miles to give a woman who paid too much her change. He became a lawyer and later was elected President. When he was President, the country was torn apart because some people wanted to end slavery and others wanted to keep it. The two sides fought each other in the Civil War. Lincoln worked with many people to end the war and put the country back together again.

After the children learn about Lincoln, they work together to tape the torn map together.

- Have you torn or broken something you wanted to keep? Did someone help you fix it?

- Do you think the President could govern the country alone? Why are lots of people needed to govern a country?

Scarcity

The things people use are called resources. Sometimes there are not enough resources for everyone. This is called scarcity. Scarcity can have many causes. For example, cold weather can harm oranges, and they can become scarce. Stores raise prices, and people have to make choices. They can either pay a high price for the oranges or buy another fruit.

Sometimes toys can be scarce too. Shoppers have to decide whether to buy a popular toy at a high price or to buy something else. In the 1970s, gasoline became scarce. People had to wait in long lines and pay high prices to get gas. Some people stopped driving cars. They walked, rode bikes, or took trains or buses. Scarcity means that people have to make choices.

- A lot of people work together to grow, ship, and sell oranges. What would happen to the oranges if people did not work together to get them to market?
- Working together can make jobs easier. Is it easier to make your bed with or without help?

The Bremen Town Musicians

An old donkey cannot work hard anymore, so he decides to go to Bremen to become a musician. On the way he meets a dog, a cat, and a rooster who join him. The animals come to a house in Bremen where they see three robbers. The hungry animals also see food on a table in the house. They decide to frighten the robbers away by singing loudly. Then the animals go into the house, eat the food, and go to sleep.

But the robbers return, and one of them wakes the cat, who scratches him, and the dog, who bites him. He then trips over the donkey, who kicks him. The noise wakes the rooster, who begins to crow. Convinced the animals are monsters, the robbers run away forever, but the animals stay in Bremen and became famous musicians.

- You sing with classmates at school. Is it more fun to sing together or alone?
- The musicians earn a living by singing together. In what other jobs do people work together?

One Good Turn Deserves Another

A mouse going across the desert sees a snake trapped under a rock and moves the rock to let the snake out. He never thinks that the snake will eat him, but that's what the snake plans to do. The mouse says, "One good turn deserves another" and the snake says he is wrong. He tells the mouse that good is often returned with evil. Then the snake says that if the mouse can find another creature to agree that one good turn deserves another, the snake will let the mouse go. The crow and the armadillo agree with the snake, but the coyote comes by and tricks the snake so it is once again trapped under the rock. The mouse runs away, and the coyote says, "One good turn deserves another."

- What is something we can do to help each other today? Is working together fun?
- The snake is not grateful to the mouse when the mouse helps him. Why should we be grateful when people help us?

Date _____

Dear _____,

Your child has just begun a new unit on Reading Street! The name of this unit is Creative Ideas. Over the next several weeks, our class will be reading about and discussing the concept of creative ideas. Throughout this unit, we will be finding out how creativity helps us communicate and solve problems, how creative ideas can bring surprises, where creative ideas come from, and other exciting aspects of creativity.

The Big Question for this unit is *What does it mean to be creative?* As we focus on this question at school, take opportunities to emphasize it at home as well. Use conversational opportunities during meals, play time, and car rides to talk with your child about the concept of creative ideas.

In this issue of *Family Talk,* you will find conversation starters, family projects and activities, and concept-related vocabulary and questions. All of these will help you and your child build understanding of this unit's concept.

Have fun!

Sincerely,

_____

What does it mean to be creative?

Concept Conversation Starters

To help your child learn about being creative, ask him or her these questions and talk about the answers.

- What is your favorite baked good? What ingredients would you use to make it?

- What art project have you done recently at school? Which materials did you use? Which colors?

- It takes creative ideas to invent something. Let's list some inventions we use every day.

- What kinds of music do we like to listen to? How does music make you feel?

Family Project

Plan a family creative project. Projects can be as varied as your own and your child's interest. You might build and paint a birdhouse, knit a scarf, sing songs for a family show, make beaded bracelets, or prepare a family favorite dish. As you and your child work on the project, talk about ways the project is creative.

Weekly Questions and Word Lists

	Pearl and Wagner: Two Good Friends	*Dear Juno*	*Anansi Goes Fishing*	*Rosa and Blanca*	*A Weed Is a Flower*
Weekly Question	When does support from others help with a creative idea?	In what creative ways do we communicate?	How can creative thinking solve a problem?	When does a creative idea lead to a surprise?	Where do creative ideas come from?
Amazing Words	construct, daydream, unique	correspond, postage, sign language	consume, shrewd, gloat	efficient, assist, generous,	excel, accomplish, research,
More Concept Vocabulary	science, conduct	electronic, speech	introduce, participate	thoughtful, share	process, apply

Selection Summaries and Questions

Pearl and Wagner: Two Good Friends

For the science fair, Pearl decides to make a robot whose mouth opens when she pulls a string. Wagner helps Pearl with the robot as he tries to decide what to make for his own project. When it's time to show their projects to the teacher, Wagner has nothing to show, but Pearl says that she and Wagner made the robot together.

On the day of the fair, the robot breaks. As Pearl leaves to get rubber bands to fix it, Wagner sees the judge coming toward him, and he climbs into the robot and begins talking. Pearl returns, and the judge asks how her talking robot works. That's when the judge looks inside the robot and finds Wagner. The friends do not win a prize, but Pearl knows Wagner wanted to help and she is glad they are friends.

- How are you being creative when you work on a science project?
- What are you studying in science? What kind of science project could you make?

Dear Juno

Juno receives a letter from his grandmother who lives in Korea, but Juno cannot read the letter because it is written in Korean. However, Juno looks at the photograph and flower that his grandmother sent with the letter, and he figures out what the letter is about. Juno decides to send his grandmother a letter. He draws pictures of his family and dog, and he adds a leaf from his swinging tree. When his grandmother writes back, she sends colored pencils, so Juno knows she wants another letter. She also sends a photograph of herself, and a toy airplane. Now he knows that she is coming to visit, and he is very happy.

- How does Juno communicate with his grandmother? Tell different ways you communicate with someone we know who lives far away.
- Grandmother came to see Juno on an airplane. How else do people travel from one place to another?

Anansi Goes Fishing

Turtle will teach lazy Anansi, the spider, how to fish, but Anansi thinks he can make Turtle do all the work. Turtle, however, gets Anansi to do the work. Turtle says that when he works alone, he becomes tired. With two of them, one can do the work, and the other can get tired. Anansi doesn't want to be tired, so he decides to work instead.

Anansi makes a net, catches a fish, and cooks the fish while Turtle rests and complains about being tired. Then Turtle says that when he eats alone, he becomes full. But now with two of them, they should share the task. One will eat, and the other will get full. Anansi wants to be full, so he lets Turtle eat the fish. Now Turtle is full, and Anansi is not. Anansi goes home upset, but he learned how to weave a net and how to catch food. He teaches all his friends how to do the same thing, and that's why there are spider webs.

- Turtle wants food. How does he get it? Why do you think Turtle tricks Anansi?
- Anansi creates a web to catch food. What do we do to get food?

Rosa and Blanca

Rosa and Blanca are sisters who help each other as they are growing up, which makes their mother very happy. Even after the sisters grow up, they still help each other. Each has a vegetable garden and decides to share the vegetables with her sister. At night each sister leaves vegetables from her garden in the other sister's kitchen. Every morning the sisters are surprised by how many vegetables are in their kitchens!

One day Rosa is home when Blanca brings vegetables to her kitchen. Now the sisters understand where the extra vegetables came from. When they tell their mother how they have been sharing, their mother is pleased that her daughters are so thoughtful. She considers herself the luckiest mother in the world.

- Rosa and Blanca surprise each other with vegetables they have grown. Have you ever surprised someone? What did you do?
- The sisters share their vegetables with each other. What can we share with someone?

A Weed Is a Flower

George Washington Carver was born into slavery, which ended when he was about ten. As a boy, he asked questions about everything. He grew plants and wanted to go to school. After he was older, he left home, worked hard, and saved his money for college. He studied agriculture in college, learning about plants and soil, and later he taught agriculture to others. Carver taught farmers to plant sweet potatoes, peanuts, and cotton. He found many different uses for these crops. Before long, peanuts and sweet potatoes were two of the most important crops grown in the state of Alabama. Many farmers and scientists contacted Carver, asking for his advice. Carver had become a well-known and respected scientist.

- Scientists ask questions and look for answers. How can they get answers to their questions?
- Carver discovered many different ways to use sweet potatoes and peanuts. Think about something, such as a cup. What are some different ways to use this object?

Date _____

Dear _____,

Your child has just begun a new unit on Reading Street! The name of this unit is Our Changing World. Over the next several weeks, our class will be reading about and discussing the concept of our changing world. Throughout this unit, we will focus on ways things change, changes in the natural world, and other exciting dimensions of change.

The Big Question for this unit is *How do things change? How do they stay the same?* As we focus on this question at school, take opportunities to emphasize it at home as well. Use conversational opportunities during meals, play time, and car rides to talk with your child about the concept of our changing world.

In this issue of *Family Talk*, you will find conversation starters, family projects and activities, and concept-related vocabulary and questions. All of these will help you and your child build understanding of this unit's concept.

Have fun!

Sincerely,

_____

How do things change? How do they stay the same?

Concept Conversation Starters

To help your child understand and appreciate the changes happening all around us, ask him or her these questions and talk about the answers.

- Think about ways you have changed. What can you do now that you could not do as a baby? How do you look different?

- Does it rain sometimes and stay sunny and warm at other times? What is the weather like today?

- We have different seasons. What are spring, summer, fall, and winter like? Which season do you like best? Why?

- Every year you are in a new grade at school. How is second grade like first grade? How is it different?

Family Project

With your child, make an album that shows changes in your family. You might use photographs, pictures from magazines, or your own drawings to depict weddings, newborn babies, growing children, grandparents, family homes, rooms that have been redecorated, and so on, that reflect changes in the family over time. After compiling the pictures, write short captions that tell about them. Then have fun going thorough the album and talking about the ways your child and your family have changed and ways that you have stayed the same.

Weekly Questions and World Lists

	A Froggy Fable	Life Cycle of a Pumpkin	Soil	The Night the Moon Fell	The First Tortilla
Weekly Question	How can familiar things help us with changes?	How do plants change over time?	What changes occur under the ground?	Why are some changes difficult?	How do changes in the weather affect us?
Amazing Words	preserve, valuable, patient	adapt, annual, nutrients	discovery, transform, underneath	adjust, foreign, unexpected	condition, predict, sparkle
More Concept Vocabulary	same, routine, different	seed, roots, leaves	minerals, humus	patch, smooth, fix	windy, downpour

Selection Summaries and Questions

A Froggy Fable

Frog is content with his life in his pond because everything is always the same. Then things begin to change: otters splash in the pond, blue jays squawk near it, and a tree crashes into the water. Frog does not like these changes.

Then one morning a boy picks Frog up, puts him in a bottle, and takes him away from the pond. Frog escapes from the bottle and tries to return home, but he is lost. When he finally finds his pond, he is happy to see the otters, blue jays, and fallen tree. He does not mind these changes after all, and he is happy to be home.

- At first, Frog does not like the changes in his pond, but then his feelings change. Tell about a time you changed how you felt about something.
- Frog's pond changes, but it remains home. Has our neighborhood changed in some ways?

Life Cycle of a Pumpkin

In spring, farmers plant pumpkin seeds in the ground. Soon roots grow down into the soil, and tiny leaves push out of the soil into the sunlight. The leaves grow, and the plants become vines that get longer and longer. The vines produce flowers that grow into little pumpkins. The growing pumpkins get bigger and bigger, and seeds and pulp grow inside. The outsides turn from green to orange, and in the fall the vines turn brown. Then it is time for the farmers to harvest the pumpkins. After the harvest, farmers plow the fields and get them ready for planting seeds again next spring. Farmers sell the pumpkins they grow, and people use them in many different ways.

- What changes take place as a plant grows?
- How much room is needed for pumpkins to grow? Why does a pumpkin farmer need more land than a green bean farmer?

Soil

Soil is a natural resource made up of different kinds of material, including tiny bits of rock, humus, air, and water. Rocks can wear away and break into tiny pieces. Part of soil is made up of tiny pieces of rocks that are minerals. The humus in soil is tiny bits of dead plants and animals.

Humus, like minerals, provides nutrients to the soil that help plants grow. Air in soil fills the spaces between the soil's bits of rock and humus. Water can move through the soil, filling the air spaces. Soil can form is some places, such as along rivers, on flat land, and on low hills, but not in others, such as steep mountains, windy places, and in rapidly flowing water. The minerals and other materials that make up soil give it different colors and textures.

- How does soil change when it rains?
- What might happen if rocks and dead plants and animals did not change to become part of the soil? Why is soil important?

The Night the Moon Fell

Long ago, Luna the Moon fell from the sky into the deep ocean and broke into pieces at the bottom of the sea. The sky turned black without her light, and the stars, birds, and flowers asked her to return, but she could not.

Luna was sad, but the fish in the sea became her friends. They began to sweep her pieces together, and they patched and smoothed them, using their scales and fins to glue them together. Now Luna could float back into the sky, and she invited the fish to join her. The fish swam up with her and began floating in the sky. That is why the moon shines in the sky, and the stars float around the moon.

- The moon's light shines in the night sky. Can we always see the moon? How does the night sky change when you can and cannot see the moon?
- The moon's shape seems to change. Let's draw pictures of the different shapes of the moon.

The First Tortilla

Jade's village is near a huge volcano, where the Mountain Spirit lives. For a long time, there has been no rain because the Mountain Spirit is unhappy with the people. The crops are dying and the lake is almost dry. A hummingbird tells Jade that she should go to see the Mountain Spirit and ask him for rain. Jade goes to the Mountain Spirit, bearing a gift. The Mountain Spirit is pleased with the gift and tells Jade he will send rain. He also gives her corn to plant. At harvest time, Jade and her parents find the corn is too hard to eat, so Jade uses it to make a special bread: the first tortilla. From that time on, the villagers grow corn and hold a harvest festival to thank the Mountain Spirit for the corn and Jade for the tortilla.

- Plants need rain to grow and change. What else do they need to grow?
- Would it be good for plants if the weather never changed? Tell why.

Date _____

Dear _____,

Your child has just begun a new unit on Reading Street! The name of this unit is Responsibility. Over the next several weeks, our class will be reading about and discussing the concept of responsibility. Throughout this unit, we will be learning why we need to do good jobs, contribute to our community, be good friends and neighbors, and be responsible people everywhere we go.

The Big Question for this unit is *What does it mean to be responsible?* As we focus on this question at school, take opportunities to emphasize it at home as well. Use conversational opportunities during meals, play time, and car rides to talk with your child about the concept of responsibility.

In this issue of *Family Talk,* you will find conversation starters, family projects and activities, and concept-related vocabulary and questions. All of these will help you and your child build understanding of this unit's concept.

Have fun!

Sincerely,

_____

What does it mean to be responsible?

Concept Conversation Starters

To help your child learn the importance of responsibility, ask him or her these questions and talk about the answers.

- What are some of our family members' responsibilities at home? What would happen if we didn't meet our responsibilities?

- What does a responsible pet owner need to do for his or her pet?

- Are you being responsible if you forget to bring home your homework? Tell me why.

- What would be a responsible thing for you to do if you dropped a dish and it broke?

Family Project

Discuss with your child his or her daily activities and the responsibilities associated with them. Then together, make a list of the daily responsibilities your child has. These may include getting up and dressed for school, eating breakfast, doing school work, brushing teeth, feeding the family pet, getting ready for bed, and so on. Create a weekly chart that places the activities in time order and has space for your child to check whether the task is completed each day. At the end of the week, review the chart.

Weekly Questions and World Lists

	Fire Fighter!	*Carl the Complainer*	*Bad Dog, Dodger!*	*Horace and Morris but mostly Dolores*	*The Signmaker's Assistant*
Weekly Question	Why should we be responsible for doing a good job?	How can we be responsible community members?	How can we be responsible animal owners?	How can we be responsible friends and neighbors?	How can we be responsible when we make a mistake?
Amazing Words	community, responsible, teamwork	concern, contribute, persuade	behavior, reprimand, obedient	appreciate, communicate, respect	apologize, citizen, judgment
More Concept Vocabulary	assistant, attitude	inquire, process	train, health	include, tolerant	correct, regret

Selection Summaries and Questions

Fire Fighter!

Firefighters work in the fire station. When the alarm rings, Liz, Dan, and Anthony slide down the pole, put on fireproof uniforms, and ride to the fire in a fire truck. An old house where no one lives is on fire, but someone saw a boy playing there this morning. Liz hooks up the hose to a fire hydrant and helps spray the fire. Dan and Anthony search for the boy, but they cannot find him. They run out of the house before the roof falls, and someone tells them the boy is safe. Later the fire is out, and they go back to the station. They are tired and hungry, but when they sit down to eat, the alarm rings again!

- Firefighters are responsible for helping to keep our community safe. What other workers are responsible for our safety?
- Tell about a task you are responsible for.

Carl the Complainer

Carl complains a lot, so his friends call him Carl the Complainer. Then he complains about the park, which he wants to stay open later. Carl and his friend Dale start a petition to keep the park open later, and they and their other friends try to get people to sign it. But no one will listen until Carl and his friends go to the park. People there are happy to sign the petition, and they get 108 signatures. The friends go to a town council meeting, where Carl makes a speech. The council members vote, and the petition works: the park will stay open later.

- Are there rules for using our park? What are the rules? How is obeying the rules being responsible?
- What things do we do that show we are responsible community members?

Bad Dog, Dodger!

Sam has a new puppy he names Dodger. Dodger is always getting into trouble. He knocks over the trash, jumps into the bathtub with Molly, chews Sam's baseball cap, and pulls down the curtains. Sam's mom puts Dodger outside, but he jumps over the fence and follows Sam to school, where he makes a mess in the classroom. Dodger runs onto the field at Sam's baseball game, grabs a bat, and runs away with it. Sam knows it is time to teach Dodger to behave. Now Sam gets up early and trains Dodger. He teaches Dodger to fetch and to stay. When he brings Dodger to a baseball game, Dodger catches a foul ball. Dodger is a good dog.

- Who is responsible for making sure a pet behaves?
- What are some other responsibilities pet owners have?

Horace and Morris but mostly Dolores

Dolores, Horace, and Morris are friends who like to explore. When Horace and Morris join a club that girls cannot join, they won't play with Dolores, who is sad. Dolores then joins a club for girls, but most of the girls don't like to explore, so Dolores quits the club. Chloris quits too, and they find Horace, Morris, and Boris, who all like to explore. The friends decide to build their own clubhouse and do things they all like to do.

- Clubs have rules. Who is responsible for making the rules? Can the rules be changed?
- Are people responsible for making sure they do not hurt their friends' feelings? What would be a responsible thing for you to do if you did hurt a friend's feelings?

The Signmaker's Assistant

Norman works for the signmaker in a town where people love the beautiful signs. Someday Norman wants to be a signmaker too. Norman makes a new "No School Today" sign that he puts on the school door. Teachers and students see the sign and go home. Then Norman puts silly new signs all over town. People get angry about the new signs and tear them all down. They think the signmaker is responsible for all the silly signs. Norman realizes he made a mistake. He is sorry, and stays up all night to make new signs to replace the silly ones. In the morning, he apologizes to everyone.

- Tell about a time you apologized for a mistake you made. How was this being responsible?
- Signs can help us know the rules. What are some rules signs tell us about? Why do we have these rules? Are we being responsible when we do what the signs say?

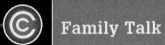
Date _____

Dear _____,

Your child has just begun a new unit on Reading Street! The name of this unit is Traditions. Over the next several weeks, our class will be reading about and discussing the concept of traditions. Throughout this unit, we will be learning about traditions in sports, national and worldwide celebrations, family parties, and traditional ways of life.

The Big Question for this unit is *Are traditions and celebrations important in our lives?* As we focus on this question at school, take opportunities to emphasize it at home as well. Use conversational opportunities during meals, play time, and car rides to talk with your child about the concept of traditions.

In this issue of *Family Talk,* you will find conversation starters, family projects and activities, and concept-related vocabulary and questions. All of these will help you and your child build understanding of this unit's concept.

Have fun!

Sincerely,

_____

Are traditions and celebrations important in our lives?

Concept Conversation Starters

To help your child understand and appreciate your family's traditions and celebrations, ask him or her these questions and talk about the answers.

- What do we do as a family to celebrate certain holidays?
- What holidays does our nation celebrate? Why are these holidays important?
- Are there foods we always eat on special days and holidays? Which foods are your favorite?
- Are there special celebrations in our community? What are they?
- Children have enjoyed some stories for a long, long time. *The Three Little Pigs* is one of these stories. Can you name others?

Family Project

Together with your child, make a list of traditions, celebrations, and activities your family participates in. You can include observances of national holidays, such as Independence Day and Thanksgiving; cultural traditions, such as ethnic foods, music, and celebrations; and family traditions, such as bedtime stories and family game nights. After compiling the list, draw pictures or gather photographs to depict the traditions. Compile the pictures into an album titled "Our Family Traditions."

Weekly Questions and World Lists

	Just Like Josh Gibson	*Red, White, and Blue: The Story of the American Flag*	*A Birthday Basket for Tía*	*Cowboys*	*Grace For President*
Weekly Question	Why are sports traditions important in our country?	What traditions and celebrations involve our country's flag?	Why are family celebrations special?	What can we learn about cowboy traditions?	How are different traditions celebrated and shared?
Amazing Words	athlete, challenge, champion	history, symbol, allegiance, patriotic	celebration, custom, tradition	legend, livestock, lariat	ceremony, culture, festival
More Concept Vocabulary	effort, practice	freedom, holiday, nation	extended family, feast, remember	rodeo, lifestyle	election, slogans, speeches

Selection Summaries and Questions

Just Like Josh Gibson

Grandmama's favorite baseball player was Josh Gibson, who was an excellent hitter. Her father saw Gibson play the day she was born and wanted his daughter to grow up to be a great baseball player too. When Grandmama was a child, girls did not play baseball. She watched her cousin Danny play, and his team let her play while they practiced. She was a very good player, and they were sorry she could not be on the team. Then when Danny hurt his arm, the team needed another player, so they let Grandmama play. She played as well as Josh Gibson, and she still has the ball.

- Children have been playing games such as Duck, Duck, Goose; hide-and-go-seek; and Ring-Around-the Rosie for a long, long time. Why do children still play these old traditional games?
- How do sports teams celebrate when they win a game or a championship?

Red, White, and Blue: The Story of the American Flag

No one is sure who created the American flag. In the 1700s America didn't have a flag, and it needed one during the American Revolution. In 1777 Congress decided the flag would have 13 red and white stripes, with 13 white stars on a blue background. At first, another star and stripe were added whenever the United States had a new state. But in 1818, Congress decided the flag would have only 13 stripes, and a star would stand for each state. Today our flag has 50 stars, and we celebrate it every June 14, which is Flag Day.

- Many people fly the flag at their homes on Flag Day. On what other days do lots of people fly a flag?
- Our country celebrates its birthday on the Fourth of July. What are some ways people in the country celebrate? What is your favorite part of this celebration?

A Birthday Basket for Tía

Cecilia's Great Aunt Tía, is having her ninetieth birthday. While Cecilia's mother gets ready for the surprise party, Cecilia puts presents in a basket for Tía. Cecilia puts in a book Tía reads to her, a mixing bowl they use to make cookies, a flowerpot, a teacup, and a ball they play with. She decorates the basket with flowers. Cecilia helps her mother get ready for the party. Family, friends, and musicians come. Tía is surprised when she gets there. She likes her presents, and she and Cecilia dance together.

- What are some birthday traditions? What does our family do to celebrate birthdays?
- People often put up decorations for birthday celebrations. What kinds of decorations have you seen at celebrations?

Cowboys

In the 1800s cowboys lived on cattle ranches in the western United States. They wore wide-brimmed hats, bandannas around their necks, and leather chaps to cover their legs. Cowboys rounded up cattle into a herd twice a year and then drove the herd to a market town to be sold. The cowboys and cattle walked on a long trail to get to a market town, and sometimes the cattle drive took months. Every night on the drive, the cook made the cowboys a meal, and then they went to sleep on the ground.

- Cowboys traditionally wore wide-brimmed hats, bandannas, and chaps. Workers in other jobs also wear special clothing. Name a job and tell what the workers traditionally wear.

- Cowboys celebrate the end of the trail drive. Think about something we celebrate. What do we celebrate? How do we celebrate? Who is part of the celebration?

Grace For President

Grace cannot believe it when her teacher says our country has never had a female President, and she decides she will be the first one. Some students laugh, but she believes she can be President.

When the class decides to have an election for school president, Grace and Thomas Cobb are candidates. Grace and Thomas have campaigns to win votes, and they make slogans, signs, and speeches. Although Grace works hard on her campaign, Thomas is not worried about winning the election because the class has more boys than girls, and he thinks all the boys will vote for him. The election is very close, but Grace wins!

- People who want to be elected traditionally give speeches. Why do you think they give speeches?

- Grace wants to break a tradition and become the President of the United States. Is there a tradition you would like to change? Why do you want to change it?

Teacher Notes

Teacher Notes

Teacher Notes

Teacher Notes

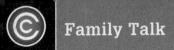
Teacher Notes